POETRY FROM SCRATCH

POETRY
FROM
SCRATCH

A Kitten's Book of Verse

Jennifer McCartney

The Countryman Press
A division of W. W. Norton & Company
Independent Publishers Since 1923

Copyright © 2016 by Jennifer McCartney

For information about permission to reproduce selections
from this book, write to Permissions, The Countryman Press,
500 Fifth Avenue, New York, NY 10110

For information about special discounts for bulk
purchases, please contact W. W. Norton Special Sales at
specialsales@wwnorton.com or 800-233-4830

Book title courtesy of Richard W. Parker
Book design by Nick Caruso Design
Manufacturing through Asia Pacific Offset

The Countryman Press
www.countrymanpress.com

A division of W. W. Norton & Company, Inc.
500 Fifth Avenue, New York, NY 10110
www.wwnorton.com

978-1-58157-428-9 (hc.)

10 9 8 7 6 5 4 3 2 1

TO OLIVIA MEOW

CONTENTS

INTRODUCTION

In central Milan, there is a lovely cat café. A space where a writer can sit and think while drinking a cappuccino out of a mug shaped like a cat. These serene writerly haunts sustain serious writers like myself. (Someone who studies literature and art and is supremely cultured.) It was on this last occasion I happened upon a small door marked "Biblioteca Gatto" I hadn't noticed on previous visits. Being the naturally curious writer that I am, I turned the small brass knob and peered inside what indeed appeared at first glance to be a small "cat library." Each volume was a slim one, and being in Italian, it wasn't quickly obvious what the volumes contained, although my excitement mounted at the possibilities. Each title was bound handsomely in leather, with gold writing on the spine and cover.

After a conversation with the owner, a kind Milanese woman named Falsa Nome, whose family had run the cat café for generations, it was revealed to me that this astonishing library contained what might be the first of its kind in the world—a repository of literature and poetry written by the cats of the café over the last hundred or so years. She and her ancestors had dutifully transcribed the cats' writings, and published them privately with a small printer in the same district as the café. It made sense to me. Italy, home to some of the world's greatest writers and artists, would naturally be home to some very intelligent and literary inclined felines. Not knowing whether

the books were of any interest to anyone but themselves, the owners of the cat café had kept the books for their own enjoyment and gradually ceased to realize the great literary importance of such a library.

I, of course, was immediately intrigued and, after many more conversations and phone calls, was able to secure the rights to translate the books into English for the first time and publish the poems abroad. Here in your hands is the first volume of that effort. A collection of the best (and only) cat poetry in existence, finally in print here for the first time. We hope you enjoy their efforts.

POETRY FROM SCRATCH

CAT VERSE INSPIRED BY FAMOUS POEMS

Classic poems are ones that we've enjoyed over the years (or studied once in high school), but, for some reason or another, are mostly lacking in cats. Here are some of your favorite poems, now with 100 percent more cats.

The Rodent Not Taken

Two rodents diverged in a yellow wood,
And sorry I could not pursue both
And being one feline, long I crouched
And watched one scurry as far as I could
To where it veered into the undergrowth;

Then took the other, as just as fair,
And having perhaps the better claim,
Because it was plump and wanted wear;
Though as for that mouse-grey hair,
Had rendered them really about the same,

And both that morning equally played
In leaves no step had trodden black.
Oh, I kept the first for another day!
Yet knowing how way leads on to way,
I doubted if I should ever come back,
to snack.

I shall be telling this with a sigh
Somewhere ages and ages hence:
Two rodents diverged in a wood, and I—
I took the one less fit and spry,
And that has made all the difference.

"Dinner" is the thing with feathers—

"Dinner" is the thing with feathers—
That perches on the windowsill—
And sings the tune without the words—
And never stops—at all—

Until—

And sweetest—in the tummy—
And sore must be Mittens—
Who couldn't catch the little Bird
That kept me full—

I've heard it in the birdfeeder—
And on the birdbath Sea—
Yet—never tasted—in its Entirety,
It left no crumb—on me.

*"A man who carries a cat by the tail learns
something he can learn in no other way."*
                              —Mark Twain

Human, This Is Just To Say

I have eaten
the herbs
that were on
the windowsill

and which
you were probably
saving
for dinner

Forgive me
they were delicious
so sweet
and so fresh

Human, This Is Just To Say

I have eaten
the Meow Mix
that was in
the silver bowl

and which
you were probably
thinking
would be my dinner

I will not apologize
it was delightful
so crunchy
and so dry

The Red Laser Pointer

so much depends
upon

a red laser
pointer

whooshing across
the carpet

I will catch it
this time

Fuzzymandias

I met a traveler from the yard next door
Who said: a vast and heavy leg of stone
stands in the garden. Topped with a bowl of water
half sunk, a flurry of sparrows bathe, whose chirps
and clueless yammerings tell of joy, and fearlessness.
They display well those passions for a summer bath—
They yet survived, our claws not stamped on those lifeless things,
Our paws that mocked them and their hearts that fed;
And on the pedestal these words appear:
"Concrete birdbath: Made in China:
Splash in me, ye mighty, and rejoice!"
Nothing beside remains, now. Round the decay
Of that colossal wreck, boundless and bare-boned
The lone and level feathers stretch far away.

O Captain! My Captain! (A Cat's Revenge)

O Captain! my Captain!
Our fearful trip to the vet is done;
My body has weather'd every shot,
the prize you sought is won;
The house is near, the birds I hear,
the neighbor's dog exulting,
While follow eyes the steady keel,
this Honda vessel grim and daring:
      But O scritch! scratch! scritch!
        O the bleeding drops of red,
           Where o'er the steering wheel my Captain lies,
             Fallen cold and dead.

As punishment.
For taking me to the vet.

Mice

I think that I must espouse
There's no meal as lovely as a mouse.

A mouse whose scar't mouth is prest
Against my furry, beating breast;

A mouse that looked for cheese all day,
And lifts her rodent arms, now, to say;

> Oh cat that may in summer wear
> A nest of robins in your hair;

> Upon whose bosom I'm now smushed;
> Who intimately nibbles on my ears.

> Please.

> Pleas are made by fools like me,
> But only you, cat, can set me free.

And so dear mouse, I let you go
A favor to you, my benevolence, shown
We live to dance another day
For now, be sure:
> Stay out of my way

*"Thou art the Great Cat, the avenger of the Gods, and
the judge of words, and the president of the sovereign
chiefs and the governor of the holy Circle; thou art
indeed ... the Great Cat."*
> *—Inscription on the Royal Tombs at Thebes*

Box

I wandered lonely as a tom
That stalked on high o'er couch and stair,
When all at once I saw an Amazon,
(A box, of golden brown)
Beside the fireplace, beneath the table,
Stoic and inviting in the spring air.

Continuous as milk and sunbeams
And toy mice that light my way,
These boxes appear in a constant stream
Full, then emptied; consumerism for another day
Along the postman's journey up our way:
Ten thousand boxes saw I at a glance,
Announcing my owner's debt, in a sprightly dance.

The favors inside them danced; but they
Once emptied, out-did the sparkling gifts in glee:
A cat could not but be gay,
In such a jocund company:
I jumped—and settled—but little thought
What wealth the box to me had brought:

For oft, when on my couch I lie
In vacant or in pensive mood,
It flashes upon that inward eye
Which is the bliss of solitude;
And then my mind with pleasure locks,
And dances with the empty box.

Do Not Stand at My Bowl and Stare

Do not stand at my bowl and stare;
The food's not there. I did not eat.
I am a thousand hours starved.
I wait and watch; the turkey's carved.
I ate the droppings on the floor.
It's not enough. Please give me more.
When you awaken in the morning's hush,
I am the swift uplifting crush
Of frantic pawing on your chest,
I am the soft meow giving you no rest.
Do not stand at my bowl and tease;
The food's not there.
I must eat—please.

Do Not Go Gentle into that Carrier for Pets

Do not go gentle into that carrier for pets,
All cats should burn and rave at close of cage,
Rage, rage against all trips to the vet.

Though wise cats, at their end, know she cares (the vet),
Because their meows had forked no lightning they
Do not go gentle into that carrier for pets.

Good cats, the last wave by, beginning to fret,
Their frail deeds might have danced in a green bay,
Rage, rage against all trips to the vet.

Wild cats who caught and ate the birds they met,
And learn, too late, they grieve freedom on its way,
Do not go gentle into that carrier for pets.

Grave cats, near death, who meow and kvetch
Sad howls could sing, be light and be gay,
Rage, rage against all trips to the vet.

And you, my owner, there on the sad height,
Curse, bless, me now with your fierce tears, I pray.
Do not go gentle into that carrier for pets.
Rage, rage against all trips to the vet.

FREE VERSE AND BEAT POETRY

These non-rhyming poems are all about cool
cats living their best lives. Creating art. Wearing
sunglasses. Riding boxcars. Best read out loud
standing up with a glass of red wine in your best
Lawrence Ferlinghetti voice.

California Cat

So cool, hanging out there on Hollywood
    Boulevard
With the tourists and the hangers on
By Mann's Chinese Theatre
The costumed superman and the
    down-on-his-luck Dora the Explorer
The cat says "no pictures please"

That cat is California cool
Might as well have a skateboard
Sunglasses
Tiny cigarette

But instead
He lounges
Sidewalk splayed
Watching the crowds, taking it all in

Dreaming of City Lights
Typing on his tiny keyboard
Finishing the screenplay
That's going to change the world

Mittens was my first true love
Her white paws were a masterpiece
Frankie was my landlord's cat
He just came with the lease

Tiger didn't like the snow
He stayed inside 'till end of May
Smokey loved her sunbeams
She'd lie in one all day

Harley was a six-toed cat
In Florida he's quite famous
Riley ate the birthday ribbon
We had to pull it from his anus

Rummy was an ancient soul
He liked to nap upon the bed
Harry loved adventure though
He often slept atop the shed

Happy was a lovely cat
She liked to purr and watch the birds
Gary wasn't potty trained
He never covered up his turds

Oscar was a mangy thing
His best friend was an alley rat
Rascal licked his red-brown tum
Sitting like the Buddha sat

Molly had a quiet nature
You could find her by the plants
Zorro loved his laser pointer
Bust it out and watch him prance

Flora was a mommy cat
She raised her litter well
Borace was a plump old thing
He looked like a big brass bell

Clem refused to use the cat door
Whining 'till you let her in
Honey was a rescue cat
We found her in the garbage bin

Now Lucy loved to lap-sit
If you were sitting—she'd be there
And Boris was a big ragdoll
He was covered in gorgeous hair

Olivia was a Calico
She ate only caviar
Little Bo was a scaredy cat
He would throw up in the car

Meow Meow clawed the carpet
And the staircase and my bed
Roxy was a Garcia fan
She was a dedicated deadhead

Angora came from Turkey
She was cultured and refined
Namaste was from Calexico
She loved yoga (just the cat pose, mind)

Neville was a London cat
His monocle was the clue
Tex was straight from Dallas
And had a taste for BBQ

Luna loved to model nude
For Friskies and Purina
Captain was less adventurous
He just hung about the marina

Angel met a violent fate
In a pet cemetery she resides
Sox was into baseball
Loved to toss that old cowhide

Peanut was a gentle soul
She liked her people quiet
Toby was a party cat
He'd be happy in a riot

Smokey was a socialist
He really felt the Bern
Malia was a Hilary fan
She felt it was a woman's turn

Coco was a fashion cat
She loved her pillbox hats
While Dexter had a murderous streak
From birds to bugs to bats

Muffin had a cooking show
She loved to bake mouse pie
While Daisy was a garden cat
The fresh catnip got her high

Casper was a ghost cat
She died in 1883
While Ziggy loved her Bowie
And dreamed of a space odyssey

MacDonald was from Newfoundland
He loved to eat cod tongue
While Sister Feline Puss Puss
Lived cloistered as a nun

Concrete Cat

```
            Ear         Ear
          Cat cat cat Cat
          Cat cat cat Cat
whisker Cat cat cat Cat whisker
            Cat cat Cat
            Cat cat Cat
          Cat cat cat Cat     tail
       Cat cat cat cat Cat      tail
         Cat cat cat Cat        tail
          Cat cat Cat tail tail
```

44

Concrete Pounce

  Ear   Ear
 Cat cat cat   Cat cat cat
EYE cat EYE   Cat cat cat cat cat   tail
Cat cat cat cat Cat cat cat cat cat cat   tail
Paw Paw Cat cat cat cat cat cat tail tail tail tail

                                    Mouse

Cat on the Union Pacific

My ancestors were mousers
On the Mayflower.
My pop's an Italian-American mouser
In Boston's North End.
And me—
A drifter. A true tom.
Left the family business
Never to return.

Domestication skipped
This generation.
So—
Put up your posters
Post the ads
I'm headed west, dear Owner.
The 3:04 to Reno
Leaves tomorrow.
I'm already gone.

The kibble, the warmth,
The quilts, the comfort—
It's not enough to keep me.

I'm headed west, dear owner.
Riding the rails,
The pot of mice at the end of the rainbow
Awaits.

Mistaken Identity

(to be read aloud while snapping your fingers and wearing a beret)

A cat
Is
Not just a cat—
snap snap snap
When
Is
A cat not a cat?
snap snap
Man
I'm telling you—
It's not
A cat
snap
When it's
Just
snap
A
Kitten

There are two means of refuge from the miseries of life: music and cats.

—Albert Schweitzer

ODES

When we think of odes, we think of the famous "Ode on a Grecian Urn," which is a serious and important poem. These odes are also very serious. They are about all the things cats seriously love: litter boxes, string, sunbeams. Enjoy!

Ode to a Fresh Litter Box

O beautiful sandy desert!
O grit mountains and hills fine!
Soft underfoot,
so fresh and so clean
—a more inviting terrain I've ne'er seen!
Now if you'll excuse me, sirs and madams,
Can I trouble you to shut the door?
I wish to explore
this walled kingdom
in peace.

*If a cat did not put a firm paw down now and
then, how could his human remain possessed.*
                                        —Winifred Carriere

Ode to a Sunbeam

I love you, sunbeam,
but must you keep *moving*?
It makes my napping
very difficult:
windowsill,
    carpet,
        armchair,
            bookshelf,
        pillow.
It's too much work.
What's this?
A cloud? No, come back!
I'm sorry, sunbeam,
Lovely warm ray of gold.
I didn't mean it.
I will follow you
Wherever you choose to go.

Ode to a Piece of String

O lithe and limber bit of string!
Forever descending,
ascending

Descending—

Ascending—

Up and away, impossible to catch
And wait!
I have you!
You're mine
To nibble and fray,
To bite and claw,
And
I'm bored now.
New toy, please.

Ode to the Corner of the Book You're Trying to Read

O firm, hardbound corner!
So good on my gums,
I rub and rub,
incessant, insatiable, constant.

Swat me away and still I return!
The corners are like catnip.
No matter what the subject—
Romance, mystery, history,
the latest Ondaatje,
Atwood,
    Franzen,
        Grisham,
Dunham—
They're all the same to me.

I will persist—
delightful, delicious corners
—until you close the book
in frustration
and turn your full attention to me.

"You are my cat and I am your human."
                —Hilaire Belloc

RHYMING VERSE, HAIKUS, AND LIMERICKS

Everyone knows real poetry has to rhyme. Otherwise, what's the point? The same goes for poems with no cats in them. Why did we even learn to read, if not to enjoy rhyming cat poetry? Enjoy some delicate haikus and some bawdy limericks, and feel free to jot down your own verse at any time. Get inspired!

Haiku of Shame

Returned from the vet
Plastic cone embarrassment
Please, please kill me now

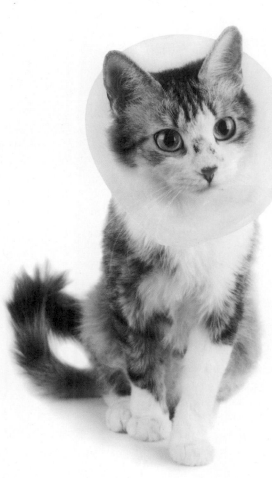

Of Mice and Men

_____

There once was a cat who loved books
He liked bookshelves that had lots of nooks
He thought especially nice
The tomes about mice
One page and the kitty was hooked

*"When I play with my cat, who knows if I am
not a pastime to her more than she is to me?"*
                    —*Montaigne*

Dr. Sturgeon

There once was a cat in a hat
(Sounds silly but that is a fact)
She ate one fish then two fish,
    a red fish, a blue fish—
The cat in the hat is now fat.

*"Two things are aesthetically perfect in the
world—the clock and the cat."*
                       —Emile Auguste Chartier

Feed Me

I'd like to file a formal complaint:
(The Ritz this certainly ain't)
My dish has been bare
Since nine past a hair!
Madam, soon I'll lose all restraint.

"Dogs eat. Cats dine."

—*Ann Taylor*

Who's Your Daddy?

There once were two cats from Carlsbad
Whose mother, it's said, was a slag.
Their father was nice,
(He loved milk, he loved mice)
But their mother's not sure he's the dad.

Cat Lady Haiku

A cat is a treat
Soft fur, a miracle of
Warm indifference

Free Ride

A cat pays no tax
A citizen of nowhere
Ruler of all things

Pirate's Booty

Ahoy mate—what's this?
A tuna can—well yo ho!
A fishy treasure

Mrs. Mittens

There once was a stay-at-home cat
Who was overworked—that was a fact.
She hired a mouse
To help round the house
(As her husband's a bit of a rat).

"My husband said it was him or the cat. . . .
I miss him sometimes."

                                    —Unknown

Cat Muse

There once was a cat from Milan
Who modeled without a stitch on.
The artists would capture
The fur-frontal rapture,
And the paintings were hung in salons.

"The smallest feline is a masterpiece."
— *Leonardo da Vinci*

STRIKING SHELTER CAT DEMANDS INCLUDE
ACCESS TO FRESH TUNA WATER,
DOUBLE THE AMOUNT OF PLAY TIME PER DAY,
AND SUNNIER WINDOWSILLS FOR NAPPING

All the cats at the SPCA
Didn't like how things ran day to day.
So the cats formed a union,
(Went on strike, paid their dues in)
And now the place runs a-okay.

"If animals could speak the dog would be a blundering outspoken fellow, but the cat would have the rare grace of never saying a word too much."

—*Mark Twain*

Royalty

I

The queen of the night is a cat.
Her fur is the blackest of black.
With a crown made of tuna
And a dog-servant named Luna,
She protects her backyard from attack

II

The king of the night is a cat.
At heart he's a true autocrat.
He dines only on mice
And everything nice
While his subjects are stuck with the rats

III

The princess of the night is a cat
But for royalty—she cares not a rat.
She instead loves to race.
In NASCAR she's an ace!
Let the record reflect she's all that.

IV

The prince of the night is a cat.
He likes to wear couture cravats.
They get lots of likes
From social media types,
Though I must add this caveat.*

*Cats don't wear ties.

Bring Your Claritin

There once was a trickster named Mack
Who liked people allergic to cats.
Upon them he'd rub,
His white mug so smug,
Till he'd trigger an allergic attack.

Wino

There once was a puss from Bordeaux
Who developed a taste for Merlot.
The cat was ashamed,
She left town, changed her name,
And now she gets drunk on Mouse-cato.

"Every life should have nine cats."
                                    —Anonymous

Catastrophe

There once was a cat named Miss Spence.
Her bonnets were really immense.
On the sidewalk she'd roam,
While the passersby groaned,
For a hat in the eye feels intense!

*"The trouble with cats is that they've got
no tact."*

—*P. G. Wodehouse*

Queen of Versailles

Look at me
A quiet, well-behaved lady writing fancy cat poetry
I'm so refined
Look at me here with my champagne
My mink throws
My editor on speed dial

Look at me with my classical education
Master's degree
Bestselling novel
I've been to Rome, you know.
It's best in the early spring, before the hordes.
And that gala last night was divine—
I don't know why the paparazzi have to be so aggressive.

Look at me
Pajama pants
Forgot to do laundry again today
Overdue credit card bills
And why does the phone company keep calling?
I told them the check is in the mail
I told them I *can't* pay online because my internet's
        been cut off
*nd now the * key is stuck on my computer.
        Gre*t. Just Gre*t.

What was I saying?
Right. C*t poetry. So refined, isn't it?
This re*lly is wh*t I envisioned.
        St*rting out. *s * young girl.
This is exactly it.

ACKNOWLEDGMENTS

Thanks to my editor Ann Treistman,
Sarah Bennett, and everyone at The Countryman
Press. Thanks Lauren Goldberg.

Thanks, cats.

PHOTO CREDITS

Cat illustrations courtesy of the author.